# Eliana

A story about a little girl who didn't get to stay.

By **A. Safiak**

# Eliana

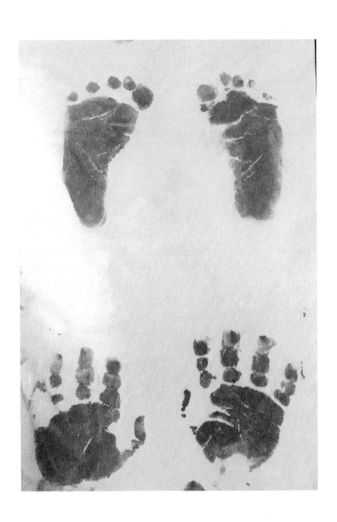

Theo's Odyssey by Catherine Clément was a book I read when I was pregnant with my first baby.

It's about a young boy who suffers from a mysterious illness and sets off to travel the world in hope of finding a spiritual cure in other faiths and cultures at the far ends of the Earth.

Somehow, years after I read it, the memory of that story resonated with me and became important when I went through a heartbreaking tragedy in my own life.

My second baby was born stillborn.

Two days before she had been scheduled to arrive in my arms alive, healthy and screaming her lungs up.

Science failed to find a reason for her death.

Someone once said to me "the genesis of a lot of things in life is random. The urge of blaming is human."

It took me a very long time to make peace with the fact that my very much wanted and loved baby had been taken away by some unexplained coincidence.

I saw and heard her strong heart at my last scan, about 5 hours before she died. Neither I nor the doctor had any concerns at that point. Everything was where it should have been and she was just perfect.

She was a big baby, had long slim fingers and toes. A cute tiny nose and a birthmark on her forehead.

My gut feeling tells me that her eyes were green after me but I do not know that for certain,
as she never opened her eyes and never took a breath outside of me.

Her name is Eliana and even though she is no longer here, I am still her mother and she is still my daughter. I love her nothing less than my other children.

She matters nothing less than my other children.
And she is a big part of me as I hope to be of hers.

I didn't have her for long but no measure of time would be enough to spend with someone you love dearly.
She was my first daughter and she was going to change this world into a better place.
Yes, she was.

There is a saying in Polish that goes: when a child smiles the whole world smiles.
So what happens when the child dies?

Despair.
Loneliness.
Longing.
Weakness.
Collapse.
Anger.
Destruction.
Destruction of faith, of love, of self, of family, of hope.

I am forever changed by the tragedy that happened to me and I am also forever defined by it as a mother and as a person.

When you lose someone who you thought would always be there, you don't just lose them once, you lose them every day.

So what do you do with your love?

Love, that despite tragic circumstances, has to find a way to manifest itself.
Love that has to find a way to speak and show.
Love that has to live.

Even though were arms are empty, I had to figure out a way to show my feelings and be proud of the impact that my daughter has had on me and others.

I will never be able to take my little
Eli for a trip around the world to cure
her from a mysterious illness but if
she is watching from somewhere I'm
sure it makes her happy that so many
people have taken her on their
journeys to the furthest ends of the
world.

To carry the memory of her,
to show respect for her short life and
perhaps to find a cure
but not for her... but... for me.
For my forever broken heart.

...

Writing her name makes her present in the minds of those who take her with them on their travels but it can also make her present in the minds of strangers, passers-by.

When they see her name written in the sand or on a piece of paper and perhaps pause for a minute and think

"What a beautiful name!"

"I wonder who this girl is?"

Or

"She must have liked it here".

...

Eli has already been carried to 6 continents and countless number of countries.

She visited the 9/11 Memorial and Museum, beaches of Morocco, Iceland, Australia, Colombia and Maldives (to mention only a few).

She was shown to the famous towers of Kuala Lumpur, brought to the green gardens of West Cork in Ireland and had her name inscribed on a rock arch in Namibia.

# MEMORIAL VISITOR
## RULES AND REGULATIONS

PROHIBITED BEHAVIOR INCLUDES, BUT IS NOT LIMITED TO:

- Expressive activity that has the effect, intent or propensity to draw a crowd, except by permission
- Demonstrations, rallies, soliciting, leafleting, promotion, and any third party vending
- Sports activities, including cycling, skateboarding, roller-blading, or roller-skating
- Loitering, littering, or smoking
- Standing, sitting or leaning on the Memorial names
- Throwing or placing anything into the Memorial pools
- Use of amplified devices
- Commercial filming, photography, or audio recording, except by permission

PROHIBITED ITEMS INCLUDES, BUT IS NOT LIMITED TO:

- Weapons, explosives, tools, and hazardous materials of any kind
- Paint and other marking instruments
- Alcohol
- Glass bottles
- Animals (except for service animals)
- Open flames
- Powdered and liquid soaps

9/11
MEMORIAL
& MUSEUM

In winter 2018, she was snuggled and carried up to nearly 8,700 meters on K2.
I dare to think that she is and will forever be the only baby who got that high up on the World's Queen of Mountain and then returned safely down, to the base camp.

She visited places that I have not and I never will.

But ultimately it is what all mothers have to come to terms with: that there are other people, sometimes strangers, who take care of our children and do what is best for them, right?

Nothing can ever take away my pain, nothing will ever bring her back to life but acknowledging that she existed, that she was waited for and cherished, makes me feel less lonely and less estranged.

LAKE
TAHOE
CALIFORNIA
USA

Eliana

Eliana died a whole life too early.
She could not leave many marks or memories behind, her time on Earth was too short for that.

But she is being loved.
She is being remembered not only by her family but by people whose hearts understand and agree to love her in the way I have chosen to show her my feelings, in the way I have chosen to heal.

I am so eternally grateful for each and every one of you.
Thank you.

Thank you so much for your kindness, your empathy and your big hearts.

Stillbirth is more common than SIDS (sudden infant death syndrome)

Sadly, it can happen to everyone.
Healthy women have stillborn babies.
Young women have stillborn babies.

Very often babies die without any reason that can be found.
Don't assume anything.
Listen.
Love.

**When meeting a bereaved parent
do not say**:

- It happened for the best

- Everything happens for a reason

- She/he was too good for this Earth

- You can have another one

- You have to move on

- Don't avoid the subject / Don't say, ask

**Instead**:

• Ask about their baby

• Tell them how sorry you are for their loss

• Say you can't imagine what they are going through

• Ask them about their baby's name

• Use the name

• Offer practical help and be patient

• Always include the baby in the family who have lost them

**Special mention to**:
(in random order)

Renia i Artur Małek

Tena O'Leary Keown

Tiarne Shaw

Beata Olech

Dominika Gołębniak

Miriam and Ruon Murphy

Manuela Mazel Kaminiarz and family

Annie and Bryan Wall

Marta Wójcik

Jagoda Mytych

Katie Sarosey Whitney

Katie Vroom

Celeste Rankine

Michelle Nerney

Żaneta Cichawa

Miriam Costelloe

David Robert Grimes

No parent should bury their child.

**I Love You Eli**
**I Miss You**
**Everyday**

Written by **A. Safiak**
Mother of four.

"Aneta has been writing poetry and prose for several years.
Some of her work has been published and received only positive appraisal.
She has a subtle but very honest and captivating style.
Her poetry dedicated profile on Social Media is highly regarded by many famous poets and writers.
She has a unique talent to convey difficult emotions into realistic descriptions.

Aneta never gives herself too much credit for her work and strongly objects to any form of approval or admiration. I have already been informed that she will not be using my full name under this note".
MK

# A letter to All Mothers
## For Mother's Day.

**Dear Mothers,**

The happiest Mother's Day is when the kids are still small and jump into your bed in the morning with homemade messy cards and cuddles.
When they come back from the crèche with chocolate buns and a tulip planted just in time in a plastic pot with the help of their teachers.
When they sing in a school show giving a less-than-perfect but IDEAL performance.

A Mother's Day lunch with your adult daughter or son is also perfect, I'd imagine.
A hamper of goodies sent from across the Ocean must bring a tear or two to a Mother's eye, I'd imagine, too.

But some of us will celebrate this day in a less perfect manner.

There are mothers out there who have lost their children.

Mothers whose mothers passed away. Mothers who are rejected and mothers who have once rejected their children, who have lost touch with their children, for one reason or another.

Mothers who are still longing for their babies. Who face the unwanted journey of infertility or loss, perhaps multiple losses.

Birthmothers.

Stepmothers.

Surrogate mothers.

I'm thinking of all of you who are wearing a dark cloak of grief on the most joyful day in the calendar. I hope you will be cherished as much as you deserve it.

I hope for empathy. I hope for kindness. I hope for acknowledgment that Mother's Day can bring a bittersweet feeling to some of us, too.
I'm holding space for all your feelings today.
I am a mother who lost her child.
I am a mother who lost her mam, too.
I see you. I hear you. You're not alone.

Printed in Great Britain
by Amazon